Before You Were Born

Retold by

HOWARD SCHWARTZ

Illustrated by

KRISTINA SWARNER

A DEBORAH BRODIE BOOK
ROARING BROOK PRESS
NEW YORK

For Miriam
—H.S.

For Sam and Sara
—K.S.

Art note: The art for this book was prepared with
linoleum printing, watercolor, gouache, and colored pencil.

Text copyright © 2005 by Howard Schwartz

Illustrations copyright © 2005 by Kristina Swarner

A Deborah Brodie Book

Published by Roaring Brook Press

Roaring Brook Press is a division of Holtzbrinck Publishing Holdings Limited Partnership

175 Fifth Avenue, New York, New York 10010

Library of Congress Cataloging-in-Publication Data

Schwartz, Howard, 1945-

Before you were born / retold by Howard Schwartz ; illustrated by Kristina Swarner.—1st ed.

p. cm.

"A Deborah Brodie Book."

Summary: Retells a folktale in which Lailah, a guardian angel, places the indentation that

everyone has on the upper lip just before a baby is born.

ISBN-13: 978-1-59643-565-0

[1. Jews—Folklore. 2. Lips—Folklore.] I. Swarner, Kristina, Ill.   II. Title.

PZ8.1.S4Be 2004   398.2089'924—dc22   2003017845

Roaring Brook Press books are available for special promotions and premiums.

For details contact: Director of Special Markets, Holtzbrinck Publishers.

First edition 2005

Book design by Jennifer Browne

Printed in May 2011 in China by C&C Joint Printing Co., Shenzhen, Guangdong Province.

4   6   8   10   9   7   5   3

One night when you were little and the moon was full, you climbed into my lap. Tell me a story, you said, about before I was born. And you snuggled closer and listened.

Before you were born, I said, your
soul made its home in the highest
heaven, in the Treasury of Souls.

The angel Lailah watched over you.
One day a heavenly voice went forth,
announcing to all the angels that the
time had come for you to be born.

Then the angel Lailah led your soul out of the Treasury of Souls and brought you down to this world.

Once you were here, Lailah told your soul to enter a seed.

Then Lailah brought that seed to your mother, and you started to grow inside her.

While you were growing there, Lailah lit a lamp inside your mother's womb and read to you from the Book of Secrets.

As you slept, Lailah taught you
all the secrets in the world.

She taught you seventy languages,
the languages of all the animals.

And the language of the wind.

She even taught you the history of your soul, and she revealed all of the past and the future to you.

Most of all, she told you
many good stories. And even
though you were asleep, you
listened to all those delightful
tales and you loved them.

Finally, the time came for you
to be born. Then the angel Lailah
led you out into the world.

But the moment you were born, Lailah put her finger to your lips, reminding you to keep everything that she had taught you a secret.

That is how you got the indentation on your upper lip. It is your reminder of all that Lailah taught you before you were born . . . and all that you have forgotten.

And you ran your finger above your lip, and, sure enough, there was an indentation there.

But don't worry, you have the rest of your life to learn all those wondrous secrets again.

This story delighted me as a child. I remember running my finger over my lip and thinking about it. Of course, I had no idea where the story came from. Only later, in my twenties, did I finally discover that this story was not merely part of Jewish folk tradition. It was a midrash found in *Midrash Tanhuma*, first published in Constantinople in 1522.

A midrash is a Rabbinic legend, and the text added some important details my mother never told me. First of all, the name of the angel was Lailah. Then I learned that when the time comes for conception, Lailah seeks out a certain soul hidden in the Garden of Eden and commands it to enter the seed. The soul is always reluctant, for it still remembers the pain of being born, and it prefers to remain pure. But Lailah compels the soul to obey, and that is how new life comes into being.

So, too, did I learn what kinds of secrets the angel taught us before we were born. As the infant grows in the womb, Lailah watches over it, reading the unborn child the history of its soul. All the while, a light shines upon the head of the child, who can see to the ends of the universe. And Lailah shows the child the rewards of *Gan Eden*, Paradise, as well as the punishments of *Gehenna*, Hell. When the time comes to be born, the angel extinguishes the light and brings forth the child into the world, and as it is brought forth, it cries. Then Lailah taps the newborn above the lip, causing the child to forget all he or she has learned. And that is the origin of the mark that everyone bears.

The story goes on to explain that Lailah is a guardian angel who watches over us all of our days. And when the time comes to take leave of this world, it is Lailah who leads us into the World to Come.

Traditions about guardian angels are found throughout the world. Some involve angels, others, like "Cinderella," speak of fairy godmothers, and still others describe spirits of the dead who guard over the living. For all of us, it is reassuring to think that there is someone who watches over us, guiding and protecting us, all the days of our lives.

—H.S.